I AM SPIRIT

POSITIVE AFFIRMATIONS

FOR

A

SOUL-FILLED LIFE

I AM SPIRIT

POSITIVE AFFIRMATIONS FOR A SOUL-FILLED LIFE

NICOLE BOWMAN

Cover Art by Nicole Bowman
www.nicolebowman.biz

DEDICATION

For the poets, healers, mystics, and wise ones.
Go within, dig deep, and believe in yourself.
That's how dreams come true and miracles happen.

CONTENTS

INTRODUCTION

Dear Reader,

I want to thank you for taking the time to purchase this book, and for utilizing it on your healing journey. I know there are many books you could have chosen, and I am honored that you selected mine. Before we move into the contents of this work, I want to share a little bit of my life story and what inspired me to write it.

My name is Nicole Bowman. I am a psychic, medium, intuitive artist, and world traveler. I have been reading professionally for over a decade. My main focus is to help people develop a spiritual practice, trust their intuition, and heal from past trauma.

I have been on a healing journey of my own for over 20 years. It began when I was an undergraduate at New York University. I was a fine arts major at the prestigious Tisch School of the Arts. Tisch was a highly competitive program that shuffled students from the classroom to Broadway and Hollywood stages each graduation year.

At the time, being a famous actor was the only conceivable option for me. It was communicated directly and covertly by my parents that I needed to have my name in lights. This would be a triumph for me and bring honor to my family. There was no negotiation and unimaginable pressure.

While I suspected that acting was not my ultimate path, I soldiered on, won awards for my craft, and received glowing reviews in news publications. I should have been happy, thrilled even, but I wasn't.

I continued to travel and work, even booking a European tour that sent me to Italy for the first time. Still, something was missing. By that time, my intuition was alive, and I knew that my spiritual growth was far more important than being famous or adored by strangers.

Throughout that period of performance, I continued to do self-love work and soul exploration. I embraced my psychic and intuitive abilities, which had always served me well when performing or creating music.

I also began to read books by spiritual workers such as James Van Praagh and Echo Bodine. Both were highly accomplished psychic mediums and spiritual teachers. Their work helped me to realize my own spiritual gifts and process the deep pain and shame I felt for no longer wanting to pursue acting and letting my family down. It was an incredibly trying time, but all the more worth it. I was healing and finding my voice.

In the midst of all this, I came across a book called *You Can Heal Your Life* by Louise Hay. It was a colorful collection of positive affirmations and musings for a happy life. Each affirmation was written in the present tense in order to draw those positive conditions into your life.

I fell in love with the book and continued to read it multiple times over. Through the years, I began to write positive affirmations of my own and when I began to read professionally for clients I would often share unique affirmations with them during sessions.

Always the avid traveler, I continued to sojourn to other parts of the globe while working remotely with clients. I continued to create affirmations for myself and share them on social media. Many people took to them and enjoyed the insights I offered.

Then, in the summer of 2018, I traveled to the island of Cyprus and began writing up a storm. To be fair, there really was nothing else to do. I could go to the beach, eat a kabob, or create. I ended up doing two out of three and emerged with a deck of homemade affirmation cards that I still carry with me to this day.

That deck was the first version of the book I am now sharing with you. I initially created those affirmations for my own healing and fulfillment. I am now giving them to you in hopes that they will assist you on your journey.

In the pages that follow, I will explain how to use this book and get the most out of the process. Always remember that healing is a journey, and nothing happens overnight. However, you can create the life you want. It just takes faith, tenacity, and the willingness to grow, one day at a time.

I wish you much love, peace, and prosperity.
You are a miracle!

In Gratitude,

Nicole Bowman
Psychic. Medium. Intuitive Artist
San Juan, Puerto Rico, 2022

How to Use This Book

There are a number of ways to utilize this book and get the most out of it. One method is to read the book in its entirety. This process will allow you to become familiar with the affirmations and exercises that are listed. Then, you can come back at a later date and explore each affirmation individually.

A second option is to set your intention for the day and ask which affirmation you need to concentrate on. Pay attention to the affirmation you are most drawn to and make it your focus for the day or the entire week.

You can also incorporate mirror work, a technique popularized by Louise Hay. In order to do this, you will need a small mirror and the affirmation of your choice. Look into your eyes and say the affirmation out loud. Affirmations may also be written on the mirror with a dry erase marker. Repeat the phrase as many times as feels necessary. The purpose is to draw those positive conditions into your life.

The final method is to complete the book in sequential order. You will see that each affirmation is numbered. There are also exercises, writing prompts, and ideas to reflect on that correspond to each affirmation.

When you see the phrase "Write It Out," this is an opportunity to write down your thoughts pertaining to the idea at hand. It can include your hopes, joys, fears, or how you best want to incorporate the affirmation into daily life.

The term "Time for Reflection" allows you the ability to sit quietly, think about the affirmation, and consider the many ways you can embody that affirmation on a regular basis.

The phrase "Time for Expression" uses activities such as dance, moving meditations, and exercise to demonstrate the affirmations through physical action.

Whichever method you choose is perfect for you. You may also create affirmations of your own, and develop new ways to embody those positive thoughts each day. See this book as a teaching tool that you can return to again and again. Every time you turn the page, you will learn something new!

THE
POSITIVE
AFFIRMATIONS

1

I AM LOVE

God is love and love is God. You can never be without them. When you believe in yourself, there is love in your life. When you believe in the divine, you have love too. It does not disappear because relationships end, shift, or change. Love is always there. Love lives inside you.

TIME FOR EXPRESSION

Take a moment to say the words "I am love" over and over again today. Write them down and say them aloud whenever you feel stressed or discouraged. Keeping those words close is a gentle reminder that you are worthy of love, and that love lives inside you.

2

I AM LIGHT

No matter how discouraging circumstances may seem, there is a light at the end of your journey. Try to understand that all ups and downs lead you to a path of power and wisdom. When darkness and confusion abound, remember that divine light shines within you.

WRITE IT OUT

Are you currently trying to see the bright side of things but finding it difficult to do so?

Close your eyes and take a moment to let go of current circumstances.

Now, ask the question: "One year from now, how do I want to feel about my life?"

As you sit with this question, pay attention to the emotions that come up. Do you feel joy, happiness, or hope? Do you experience excitement, contentment, or peace?

This is the direction you want to move in. Allow the emotions to flow through your body and enjoy the sensation. When you are ready, open your eyes and take a moment to write about what you felt.

Record as much as you can, and embrace those positive feelings.

The more you live in that space, the more you will be able to envision it on a daily basis. Even if your current life doesn't reflect those experiences, this process will help you to understand that change is possible.

With time, this process may also inspire you to take real-world actions, plans, and steps to reaching your dream. It often starts with being able to feel and envision that new life.

Take some time to write down what you just experienced,
and explore that now.

3

I AM JOY

Now is the time for friends, family, and celebration. Always remember to rejoice and smile. Laugh openly. Enjoy these sweet moments. Connect deeply with others.

TIME FOR REFLECTION

As you go about your day, reflect on what brings you joy in the present moment. Pay attention to conversations, interactions, and simple occurrences that fill your heart with light. Look for the joy in those experiences, and watch it rise inside of you. The more you are open to it, the stronger it becomes.

4

I AM PEACE

Listen to the beat of your own heart and breath. This is how you learn to be still. Things are working out in your favor. Trust the process. Choose peace.

TIME FOR REFLECTION

All you need is 5 minutes to do this brief exercise. Grab a comfortable chair and have a seat. Place your feet firmly on the floor and close your eyes. Breathe in through your nose, and out through your mouth. Let your worries and cares slip away as you follow the rhythm of your breath.

When thoughts come up, try not to examine them or judge them. Just let them flow in and out, establishing a sense of peace and stillness within you. Continue to follow your breath for a little while longer, and when you are ready, open your eyes.

Then affirm, "I am peace," out loud. You can say this affirmation throughout the day, verbally or telepathically. It's great for times when life gets busy and you need a reminder to breathe and slow down.

Peace is always possible.

5

I AM GOD

God is never outside of you. God lives in your heart. The divine blueprint that exists within the cosmos resides within in you. Never doubt that God has your back. Trust in the divine.

TIME FOR EXPRESSION

As you move through the day, repeat the affirmation, and try to remind yourself that God is always on your side. Whenever you feel anxious or discouraged, repeat the words, "I trust the process. God has my back." This allows you to acknowledge what you are feeling while simultaneously knowing that everything is working out in divine order.

6

I AM GODDESS

The divine is both masculine and feminine. One cannot exist without the other. Embrace your feminine energy today. Learn when to be silent, when to study, and when to act. Take in all necessary information before making a decision. Move slowly, move wisely, and then, move decisively. You will be victorious.

WRITE IT OUT

Take a moment to write out your tasks for the day. As you reflect on the list, begin to ask yourself which tasks are most important. While reflecting on them, scan the list and see where you fall.

Are you putting things on the list that make you a priority?

Are you including things that nurture your body, mind, or spirit?

In the hustle and bustle of life, it is always important to include your personal happiness.

If you do not find yourself anywhere on the list, consider adding something that honors you. This could be a scheduled break during the day or your favorite food for dinner. This could be taking time to rest or watching a program you love later in the day. The point is to acknowledge you inner goddess. Nothing is too big or small. Trust what you are feeling, and let your inner knowing lead the way.

7

I AM SPIRIT

The human experience is a beautiful one, but we must never forget that we are spiritual beings in human form. Remember that you are eternal, and today's dramas and worries will soon be over. Try not to stress over small things. Focus on the bigger picture, and spend your time, energy, and thoughts on what truly matters. This will feed your spirit and enrich your soul.

WRITE IT OUT

What is the one thing that you want to accomplish today? It doesn't have to be important to the world. It needs to be important to you. Think of the one thing that will give you satisfaction at the end of the day. One thing that will quiet your mind and allow you to rest easy. Once you have it, write it down and schedule it into your day. Sometimes, it's the little things that honor your spirit.

8

I AM AIR

It is wonderful to set goals and manifest them. However, at a certain point, we must let go. We must dream the dream, do the physical work, and leave the rest up to God. Once you have done all you can, it is time to allow spirit to work its magic. What is for you will be for you. Simply know that, and let spirit guide the way.

TIME FOR REFLECTION

We all have moments where we feel stuck. Maybe it's a relationship that's not working or a job that is stressing us out. There are moments when we have given all that we can, and there is nothing left to be done. The rest is up to the divine.

If you are currently experiencing this, it may be necessary to stop trying to fix it, and understand it will fall into place when the time is right. Perhaps there is nothing more to do than realize things will unfold for the highest good. Consider stepping away from the problem, and realize that circumstances are temporary. You are spirit, and what is best for you will always find its way home.

9

I AM HOPE

Things often look darkest before a new beginning. That is why we must persevere and keep going. Have hope for the future. Have hope that new and beautiful things are on their way. Just because you can't see them, doesn't mean they are not coming. In fact, they may already be here. You just have to shift your perspective.

WRITE IT OUT

Can you recall a specific time when things in your life seemed to be falling apart, but they were actually coming together in the most unexpected way? Take a moment to reflect on that now, and record your experience.

10

I AM HERE

It's time to take up space in this world. Know you are worthy of the hopes, dreams, and leadership positions that await you. You are deserving of great blessings. Now is not the time to shrink and hide. Stand up tall, be proud, and know that you are worthy.

WRITE IT OUT

How are you showing up in the world?

Is there a talent or gift that you have been hiding?

If you knew things would work out well, what would you do?

What dreams would you pursue?

How would your life look differently now?

It's time to consider that. The possibilities are endless.

11

I AM WISE

There is a still, small voice that guides you, and a brilliant intellect that leads the way. You know what to do. Never doubt that the answers are there. They are waiting to be discovered, waiting to be uncovered. Deep inside, you know the truth, and it will set you free.

TIME FOR REFLECTION

Think back to a time when you knew in your heart that you needed to complete a certain task or make a clear decision. Maybe you realized you needed to end a relationship, apply for a new job, or have a difficult conversation with someone you loved. Either way, you felt deep down in your soul that action was necessary.

Take a minute and recall that moment now.

How did you feel inside when it was apparent you needed to make a move?

Did you feel it in your gut?

Did you simply have a knowing?

Was there a stirring inside calling you to action?

Explore that feeling now, and try to remember it. That is the feeling of inner knowing. It is the eternal part of you guiding the way. Once you recognize what that sensation feels like, you can apply it to all areas of life when making important decisions.

12

I AM MUSIC

Your life is a symphony, and each experience is like an instrument that plays its part. Even periods of silence are a part of the song. Learn to trust the process. Learn to appreciate the harmonies. Each sound is a part of a greater journey.

TIME FOR REFLECTION

Focus on a time in your life where you wanted something so badly but it didn't work out. Examples could be a relationship, admission to a school, or material success. At the time it probably felt like things were falling apart and the world was an unfair place.

However, with time and distance, perhaps you saw why things didn't work out and began to realize that what happened was for the best. What transpired was a part of your story. It was the soundtrack to your life, and even though things felt broken at the time, they were actually fitting perfectly into place. Try to remember this the next time you don't receive what you want. Maybe it's not a part of your purpose; maybe you have a greater song waiting to be sung.

13

I AM ART

You are a masterpiece. Your life and experiences are art made manifest. Even your perceived flaws and blemishes are a part of the divine tapestry. Never forget your brilliance. Hold on to the light.

WRITE IT OUT

What is your gift?

Is there something you possess that makes you unique?

It could be an obvious talent like singing, dancing, or mathematics. It could be something more subtle like being able to cheer people up, inspire others, or lead a team to victory. We all have a gift that is uniquely ours. It allows us to be artists and creatives in our own right because no one can do it the way we do.

If you ever feel like you don't fit in or feel like you have nothing to offer, look to your gifts. Even the small ones make a big difference in this world. They are your contribution to this beautiful mosaic called life. Your presence makes a difference. Remember that.

14

I AM WORTHY

Open your arms wide and accept the divine gifts that flow into your life. Love, peace, and joy are within your reach. You are worthy of happiness. You are worthy of great success. You are meant to live your best life, one that fully reflects your potential.

TIME FOR REFLECTION

Are you currently doubting your worthiness? Do you question your ability to have success and get the job done? Maybe you are in a workplace, relationship, or time in your life where things seem out of sync. Maybe you feel like you are out of your depth.

During times like this it is important to remember that you are in the right place at the right time. You deserve to take up space in this world. The blessings and opportunities that come your way are for you. Whenever you feel discouraged, say, "I am worthy," out loud or telepathically. It is a gentle reminder that where you are is where you need to be.

15

I AM SHADOW

Light cannot exist without darkness. Things that are hidden must be brought into the light. Do not hide the less evolved aspects of yourself. Do not bury the parts of your life that appear to be imperfect. It is through our imperfections that we become unique. It is through our weaknesses that we learn and grow. Light and shadow go hand in hand. There is love, there is light, and there is darkness. All are valid. All are holy.

TIME FOR REFLECTION

We all have weaknesses, character flaws, and personal hang-ups. These qualities do not have to define us, but they can give us insight into what we need to work on. They are also a gentle reminder that we are human and that part of this life is recognizing that we don't know it all but we are open to learning.

You don't have to be perfect to make a difference in this world. Whether you are struggling with addiction, feelings of insecurity, or emotional instability, please try to understand that all of these things can be a part of the human experience. The key is not to hide them, but to understand that in spite of that, you are a perfectly good human being. Everyone has a struggle, everyone has darkness. It is important to embrace it, affirm we deserve love, and keep living openly. That is when magic happens.

16

I AM HEART

Give your all to what you believe in, no matter how bleak things may seem. If you have a dream, hold it in your heart and push forward. Keep going, keep creating, keep evolving, but most importantly, keep living.

WRITE IT OUT

Dreams work when we do. They come true when we write them down, put dates on them, and put a plan in action. Take a moment to reflect on the year ahead. Where do you want to be at the end of this year emotionally, financially, or spiritually?

Then, take a moment to determine how you will get there.

What physical steps do you need to take in order to make this dream a reality?

Break it down month by month and put dates on your goals.

With time you will see your dream unfold, and the future will become your reality.

17

I AM THANKFUL

There are so many things to be thankful for. So much to rejoice about. Sometimes, it's the small things; your morning coffee or how the sunlight streams through your window. Other times, it is bigger things; falling deeply in love, traveling the world, creating the life of your dreams. No matter how large or small, there is always something to be thankful for.

WRITE IT OUT

Look for the blessings, look for the little things. Writing them down can be a wonderful reminder. Make a list of things you are thankful for today, no matter how big or small. When you put them together, it's a great big life.

18

I AM AWAKE

See things as they are, not how you want them to be. Viewing life with a clear set of eyes allows us to accept the truth and make sound decisions. Explaining it away or denying what is in front of us only further buries our intuition. When our eyes are wide open, and we gaze at the world with no filter, it allows us to witness the truth.

TIME FOR REFLECTION

Take a moment to recall a time in life where you were in denial about something that was inevitable. Perhaps it was time to make a move or a career shift, or accept that the circumstances of a relationship had changed. Maybe you were struggling to accept the truth, but deep down you knew what was happening.

Moments like this are teaching tools. They teach us to accept what is, and to embrace what is true. We don't have to like it. The point is not to like it. The point is to accept it. When all roads point to one door closing, another will open. It's time to listen.

19

I AM EARTH

You are meant to be on the planet at this time. You have a very special purpose. The Earth is here to support you and nurture you so that you may fulfill that purpose. In turn, you protect and love the Earth. Continue to look inward and remain grounded. Try not to get swept up in the emotions, hysteria, or chaos occurring around you. Trust in the Earth. Trust in yourself. Both will keep you steady.

TIME FOR EXPRESSION

When everything is changing around you, when everything feels chaotic, silently affirm that it will all work out. Know in your spirit that things are working out for the highest good. They may not happen immediately, but they will unfold eventually. If you feel unsteady, silently affirm, "I am Earth." It is a reminder that you are supported, and any battle that comes your way, you will get through.

20

I AM FREE

You are free as the spirit that dances inside you. You are free as the wind, flowing and traveling. You are not trapped. You are not broken. You are not stuck. You can always begin again. You can always start over. Continue to open your mind and cultivate the connection to spirit. Allow those energies to come forward and carry you where you need to be. Your spirit is free, vibrant, and alive. Nothing can hold you down. Many beautiful things are possible.

WRITE IT OUT

If you could do anything and not experience failure, what would it be?

Would it include a career change?

Telling a person how you truly feel?

Moving to a new place?

Our spirit knows no limits or bounds. It isn't confined to what the world tells us or how the world defines us.

When you write down dreams and goals, write them from a place of possibility, not limitation. Don't censor yourself. Let your imagination run wild. If something is truly yours, you will find a way to make it happen.

It may not be easy, but you will move past obstacles. Do not limit yourself. Dream big and watch how things fall into place. Remember, you don't need all the answers at once. They will come in time.

21
I AM WATER

Water takes the shape of anything it flows into. It travels, it bends, it adapts. Be flexible like water, and watch your life change. When we are flexible, obstacles can become opportunities. Dead ends can become open doors. There is always a way through the impediments that appear to block our good fortune. We just have to be like water, think creatively, and go with the flow.

TIME FOR REFLECTION

Have you ever experienced a time when nothing seemed to go right? You prayed, hoped, and wished for something better, but doors seemed to close all around you? No matter how hard you worked, it was never enough. In fact, the harder you pushed, the more difficult life became. Have you ever considered what that period of time was trying to teach you?

Sometimes, we need to slow down and allow things to happen the way they need to. We have done the hard work, and we simply have to wait for the outcome to unfold. There are also moments where the outcome we want is not the best one for us, and the more we resist, the more difficult our life can become.

There are moments where we just need to stop and accept what is happening. Oftentimes, it is not the end of our story. We are somewhere in the middle, waiting for things to come together. We do not have to burst through every locked door. Sometimes, it is locked for a reason, and there is something better on the way.

22

I AM HEALING

Healing takes time. It is a daily process. Try not to rush yourself or compare your healing path to those of others. Move at your own pace, embrace the journey, and allow life to unfold in a way that is best for you.

TIME FOR REFLECTION

Healing is both miraculous and mysterious. Sometimes, it occurs instantaneously, and we are immediately transformed. Other days it takes an extended period of time, and we must learn patience and how to build our faith. It is important to know that we each have a healing journey all our own, and however long it takes is what is necessary for us.

Sometimes, prolonged healing is the key to spiritual growth. It allows us to trust ourselves and our higher power. It allows us to reflect on what we wish to do differently and how we want to live. Moreover, healing doesn't always mean that the issue, whether it be physical, emotional, or spiritual, is fully eradicated. It means that the way we look at it has changed. And because we look at it differently, we react to it differently.

Consider a time in your life where healing was needed. Perhaps a relationship ended or there was a health problem you were experiencing. Did those issues resolve themselves immediately or did they take more time? What did you learn from the experience? Did it teach you self-love, care, and healthy boundaries? Did you learn to trust your intuition when making life decisions? Was it a wake-up call to listen to your body and honor it?

As you can see, all these lessons help promote healing because they aid in our spiritual growth and awareness. They allow us to see difficult experiences with a new set of eyes and embrace the bigger picture.

It is important to note that healing does not always mean that the condition or circumstances have changed. However, healing does mean that you have changed and, with time, have evolved into a clearer, purer version of who you truly are.

23

I AM WHOLE

Wholeness does not come from the outside world. We don't acquire it through material possessions or even the love, affection, and admiration of other people. Wholeness comes from within. It is birthed when we decide to take up space in the world and pursue our dreams. No one else can give us that. We must give wholeness to ourselves.

TIME FOR REFLECTION

Take a moment, in this quiet space, to observe your surroundings and breathe. Whether you are at home, at work, or out in nature, you are existing peacefully in this space. The past is gone. The future has yet to be determined. All you have is the present moment, and in this moment you are perfect, whole, and complete. Take a moment to savor that truth, honor the solitude, and breathe.

24

I AM LIFE

As long as there is breath, there is life. You are a beautiful expression of life and love; filled with color, light, and endless possibilities. Speak on what you desire. Call it into existence and walk with courage. Envision yourself thriving as the world opens up. Speak life into what is most important. Watch it grow, and celebrate the beauty and miracle of being in this world.

WRITE IT OUT

If there is one thing you want to do before you leave this planet, what would it be?

Is there someone you need to make amends with?

A trip you need to take?

A book you need to write?

Take a second and reflect on that now.

Then, write it all out on the page, without limitations or restrictions. Write your life, write your dreams, write your story. Write about the one thing you know you must do.

Feel it in your soul. Life is just beginning. Your future has yet to be written.

25

I AM REBIRTH

There is life, there is death, and there is rebirth. It is a sacred cycle that prepares us for new pathways. Doors may close, but it's not always goodbye. Sometimes, it's an opportunity to say hello. Hello to a new way of being. Hello to new experiences. Hello to new people and adventures who will change our lives for the better. Allow yourself to rise up and see the beauty of a new day.

TIME FOR REFLECTION

Are you holding on to a piece of the past that is bearing no fruit? Despite the desire to hold on, is it time to let that go? Yes, change is difficult, but it is necessary for our growth. Part of rebirth is learning when to let go, and realizing what we need to let go of. If there is anything unnecessary that you are holding on to, vow to let it go. Take time to reflect on that now.

26

I AM TRUTH

Speak what is true. Let honesty and light fill your inner being. Chant the words that calm your soul. Speak with integrity and clarity. Tell the truth, live the truth, walk the truth. Do not lie to yourself. See life as it is and learn to accept it.

TIME FOR REFLECTION

Do you say what you mean and mean what you say? Do you hide your feelings or speak in code, hoping that other people will anticipate your needs? Maybe it is time to say exactly what you mean, state exactly what you need, and let the chips fall where they may. The people who are able to meet your needs will meet you where you are. Others will fall away. When all else fails, speak the truth. It will save you and chase away any confusion you may be facing.

27

I AM DIVINE

You are both human and spirit, part of this magical tapestry that dances on planet Earth. You come from the stars, and your presence has great power. There is always a divine energy that flows around you and inside of you. It offers protection, inspiration, and comfort. This energy can never leave because you are divine. Recognize your brilliance, and step into your power.

TIME FOR EXPRESSION

Look in the mirror today, stare into your own eyes, and say, "I am divine. I am eternal. No matter how dark or heavy things appear to be, I triumph, I rise above, and I live on."

Quietly affirm those words as you move through the day.

You are eternal.

You live on.

You survive.

28

I AM MAGIC

Magic does not exist outside of you. Magic lives within you. You have the ability to transform your life. Transform your reality. Never doubt the fortitude of your own power. You are alive, brimming with magic, brimming with hope. Say yes to positive changes.

TIME FOR EXPRESSION

Look for the miracles today. Look for the magic. Look for the synchronicity that flows together, letting you know that things will be alright. Say a silent prayer that everything will come together. Magic unfolds when you expect it to work. Affirm your success today, and watch for the little signs that it is unfolding.

29

I AM STARDUST

When we cross this earthly plane, we all return to the stars. We are a part of the cosmos. If you ever feel alone, ever feel lost within the world, look up at the stars. That is your home, and one day that is where you will return.

TIME FOR REFLECTION

Are there loved ones in spirit whom you miss? Do you ever feel like they are so far away and out of reach? When the sun goes down, take some time to step outside and look up at the stars. Reflect on the happy times, the powerful memories, the joy you shared. Know and understand that they are never too far away. You are a part of them, and they are a part of you.

To the stars and light you will return someday.

Until then, continue to live and honor their legacy by walking in

YOUR LIGHT!

30

I AM FIRE

Fire is transformative. Through fire, we are reborn. If you are currently experiencing trials and tribulations, understand they will not last. You are being refined. You are being fortified, and just like the phoenix who rises from the ashes, you are being reborn.

TIME FOR REFLECTION

Are you trying to hold on to the past? Are you fighting for something that no longer exists or yields positive results? Have you prayed for a successful outcome but to no avail? Maybe it is time to let it burn. Maybe the answer to your prayers is to let it all fall down, collapse, and allow yourself to be reborn.

Miracles happen when we stop fighting and embrace the change. Lay your burdens down and step into the fire. Through the embers you will be transformed, healed, and bathed in light.

31

I AM HOLY

God does not live outside of us. God lives within us. We are holy. Holy in our flesh, holy in our spirit, holy in our minds. We are children of the divine. A physical expression of divine brilliance and godliness. We are children of the most high.

TIME FOR EXPRESSION

Have you ever experienced the morning light? Do you know what it is like to wake up at sunrise and be alone with your thoughts? Take a day this week and wake up at dawn. As the sun fills the sky, thank God for your life. Thank great spirit for your divinity, and as you begin your day, know that you are one with the creator who sent you.

Silently affirm,

"I am holy,"

throughout your day.

32

I AM GROWING

Growth is a part of life. During our walk on this planet, we may outgrow many things, from relationships to schools of thought to religious views. When this happens, give yourself the grace and permission to change. This process is a part of life. It is a sign you are living authentically, enjoying the seasons, and embracing your soul's evolution.

WRITE IT OUT

Take a moment to reflect back on a strongly held belief that you no longer subscribe to. Now, consider how long it took for that belief to change. It may help to write the process down. Maybe you held certain religious or spiritual beliefs that no longer serve you. Perhaps you had political views that do not currently support the life you are creating. Maybe you left a relationship that you thought would be your forever.

Did the shift occur in weeks, months, or years?

What led you to embrace the change?

What emotions did you experience before, during, and after the shift?

Moreover, how has your life changed for the better since you made your choice?

Take that memory and write it down.

Doing so illustrates that you can always start over, and that beginning supports a brand new you.

33

I AM HARMONY

Everything in life has its perfect timing. It's not so much about having everything at our fingertips right when we want it. It is more about having the necessary things when we need them. Learn to appreciate what flows in and out of your life. Try to envision that flow like a piece of music. Each instrument, each voice, has its part. From the percussion to moments of deep silence. When they come together it tells a greater story. The majestic sounds blend and melt with ease. It all makes up a beautiful life. Trust in that. Your time is coming.

WRITE IT OUT

Starting your day with a schedule can be liberating. There is often a freedom in structure. First thing in the morning, take some time to write out your daily routine. Whether it be work, fitness, or spending time with your family, create a schedule that supports and includes what is most important to you. Now, as you move through the day, refer back to the schedule and try to adhere to it if you can.

However, be mindful that schedules change and things can come up. As you move through your day, you may have to shift things around and adapt. Maybe the work meeting goes longer than expected, so your workout happens later. Perhaps the dinner you were planning has to be takeout instead.

The point is to understand that changes happen, and even with the best-laid plans, we still need to go with the flow. When we have a schedule there is a basic structure we can always reach back to, but the harmony comes when we learn to accept the unexpected changes and make time for what matters as we are able to.

Sometimes, we have to get in where we can fit in. As long as we try to make room for what is most important, we are in harmony, we are in flow. One off day is not the end of the world. It is what we do consistently and what we make time for (no matter how small) that matters.

34

I AM THRIVING

You are moving from a space of simply surviving to thriving. But in order to get there, we must let go of the past. We must let go of things that are no longer working. This may include past relationships or mindsets that no longer serve us. In order to thrive, we must become lighter and let the baggage go. What do you need to release? What have you been clinging onto? Let the dead weight fall away, and affirm your new life.

TIME FOR REFLECTION

Identify one thing in your life that is no longer working. Maybe you have been putting energy into this for a long time. It could be a relationship that continues to go off the rails. No matter how hard you try, you never seem to reach common ground. It could be a business venture that is not yielding any positive results. It could also be unrealistic goals that you need to release in order to move forward.

Thriving happens when we begin to travel lighter. Once we realize certain things are not working and turn our attention to what is possible, we let go of the struggle and we begin to level up. Sometimes, the way to thrive is to release.

35

I AM REJOICING

There is beauty in every day. Sometimes, it comes from simple things, like watching the sunrise or having a cup of coffee in the morning. Rejoice and be grateful for the life you have. Give thanks for the simple pleasures. This makes way for new blessings and beautiful memories that are yet to come. Your story is not over yet. Rejoice, live, and grow!

WRITE IT OUT

This week, commit to writing down one thing you are thankful for every day. It can be something very simple. It just has to be important to you. As you focus on what you appreciate, you will begin to feel more abundant. You will naturally shift your focus to what is working in life versus what is not.

When we focus on what we love, we feel uplifted. When we focus on the blessings in life, we start to feel more prosperous. Doing so raises our mood and gives us the energy to move forward. Look for the good this week. Search for the tiny blessings that make life worth it.

36

I AM MULTI-DIMENSIONAL

You are a multifaceted being. Your mind, body, spirit, race, sexuality, and unique talents are all parts of the divine essence that flows through you. Each one is important, but no piece completely defines you. They allow you to show up in the word and be seen. They allow you to connect with spirit and realize there is life beyond this physical plane. Embrace your differences and embrace the many aspects of you. Honor them all. Celebrate every part of your being, no matter how ordinary or mundane it may seem. This celebration and acceptance is an act of divine love.

TIME FOR EXPRESSION

Take some time this week to explore a hobby or interest that you normally don't focus on but have always wanted to try. This could be a yoga class, painting, or exploring a new genre of music. The point of the exercise is to open up different channels within yourself for creative expression.

When we try new things, we are open to the many different facets of our soul. It reveals new talents and strengths. We begin to see different sides of our personality that we never knew existed. It helps us to understand that we are more than our bodies. We are spirit, and as we listen to the stirrings inside, it allows our true essence to shine.

37

I AM HEALED

The weight you are holding is no longer yours to carry. Lay your burdens down. Let go of what has hurt you, and release your old identity. Open up to the promise of something new. Healing is about clearing away the cobwebs of life and seeing clearly once more. Let the labels go. Let the past go. Let all judgments be erased and heal.

TIME FOR REFLECTION

Consider this: Healing doesn't mean that the pain never existed. Healing means you are willing to accept the past and make peace with it, even though it was less than perfect. You are willing to let go. By letting go, you free yourself up for new experiences.

Is there something or someone you need to release today?

Have you been holding on for far too long?

Healing happens when we make space for what matters.

We may have to do this by clearing out what doesn't.

What do you need to let go of today?

What is the first thing that comes to your mind?

That's your answer, and you don't have to know how to let go.

You just need to be willing.

38

I AM BLISS

You are moving at the speed of light. In love with life, in love with the divine, and certain of your own luminosity. Bask in the joy and bliss of life. Look for beauty and happiness everywhere you go. It is all around you. This is how you live your bliss.

TIME FOR REFLECTION

As you go about your day, look for the beauty in things and find something to be grateful for. You may find this out in nature, or within the comfort of your family. You may notice it at work, or in the arms of your significant other. It is the little things we notice, tiny little threads stitched together, that make a great big life. It could be a piece of art, a sunset, or a warm hug. It could be the way the breeze feels on your skin. Look for the beauty today, and you will find it.

39

I AM EVOLVING

You are not the person you were yesterday, the day before that, or even a year ago. You are growing in wisdom and knowledge. You are learning to be more accepting of yourself. You are allowing in ideas that challenge you and force you to question who you are. That is a sign of evolution: to level up and recognize that what you once believed may no longer be true for you. However, the previous belief served its purpose in the moment. The experience helped you to evolve.

WRITE IT OUT

We are always evolving. Take some time to reflect on how far you have come, and take a moment to write it down.

Is there something you once believed that you no longer hold true?

Was it a limiting belief about yourself or others?

Was it a barrier put in place that blocked your success?

Think about one thing you once believed that is no longer true for you.

Write it out in great detail. Through this process, you will see how much you have overcome. If you can change and evolve, others can too. In growth and evolution there is hope. Believe in that.

40

I AM CHANGING

Everything changes, and part of life is accepting that change. Learning to go with the flow, releasing old mindsets and experiences, it is all connected to new beginnings. Change is also a part of the evolutionary process that is integral to our spiritual growth. Nothing stays the same. There is beauty in change, beauty in great shifts. Try not to resist it. Allow yourself to flow.

TIME FOR REFLECTION

Try not to force anything today. Be a quiet observer. Watch what happens around you and notice things shift and change. Pay attention to conversations and interactions between others. Try not to interfere. Things often come to their natural conclusion if we allow the changes to happen without force.

41

I AM BREATH

Breath has the power to give life, and breath has the power to release what is no longer necessary. Give breath and voice to what you love. Give breath and voice to what you want. Release with breath that which you no longer need. See it as a cycle, a beautiful give and take. A process of creation, a process of destruction, a process of rebirth. Lead with the breath.

TIME FOR EXPRESSION

In times of stress today, learn to use your breath. Breathe in through the nose and out through the mouth. While breathing out, exhale the negativity, the pain, and the doubt. Let it drift away from you.

As you inhale, breathe in hope, joy, and dreams. Allow those positive energies to flow into you. Whenever you are scared or stressed, try this exercise. It slows you down and allows life to flow.

42

I AM POWER

Step into your personal power. The time is now. There is no need to shrink or hide. Be bold. Have pride in who you are. Own your power.

WRITE IT OUT

Is there a dream or goal you have yet to accomplish?

Are you afraid that you might not succeed?

Take some time to write that dream out in great detail today. Then, read your words out loud. Allow your dream to seep into your spirit and permeate your being.

Now, take a moment to consider: What physical steps do you need to take in order to make this dream a reality?

Begin to write them down.

This is the first step to owning your power. Have the courage to speak into existence what you want and the bravery to stand up and make it happen.

That is power.

43

I AM FLYING

Far above the clouds there is a place that is eternal. It is our spiritual home. It is a place where there are no limits. We can take that limitless energy and apply it to life here.

WRITE IT OUT

Let's take a moment to strip away your outer appearance. Remove race, sex, gender, nationality, and politics from the mix.

Who are you without these labels?

What words would you use to describe your true essence?

What do you believe in?

What is most important and precious to you?

When the outer labels fall away, the soul remains.

Take some time to write that out now, and see what new worlds you discover!

44

I AM DANCING

Dancing opens up the soul and connects us to spirit. Life itself is a dance. Sometimes we lead, sometimes we follow, and other times, we stand still, waiting for the music to inspire us and guide us home. We just have to remember not to stand still too long. Everything moves in its own time with perfect pace and rhythm.

TIME FOR EXPRESSION

Put on a piece of music today, any kind of music, and allow your body to flow with the rhythm. Don't think about how you look or whether or not you can dance. Allow your body to move and sway. Allow it to express your joys, fears, and pain. Allow it to stretch and bend as your heart connects with sound. Movement is powerful. It heals us. It frees us up. It unlocks our creativity.

45

I AM BALANCE

Take your time with everything. Understand that everything has its own rhythm and cycle. Life is not about perfection. It is about doing things in the right sequence for you. When we surrender to the flow of life, we create more balance in our lives. We don't have to do everything all at once. Do things as needed.

WRITE IT OUT

Having a schedule can keep us on track, but being too rigid can make life less enjoyable and less productive in the long run. When you sit down to plan out your day, consider that. Instead of making a list of all the things you must do, look at what is most pressing. Do that first.

Then, think of something you would really like to do. Something fun and exciting that is just for you. Put that down on the list as well. In doing so, you may find that everything demanding your attention is not an emergency.

Balance comes when we recognize what is important and try to divide our time between work, play, and relaxation.

46

I AM OPEN

Amazing things can happen when we let go of expectations and allow the universe to surprise us. Sometimes, there is power in not knowing. It opens us up to more opportunities. Opportunities we could never dream of. Yet those experiences fit perfectly into the life we are creating. Sometimes, we have to let go of the picture in our minds to give way to an even more brilliant future.

TIME FOR REFLECTION

Have you been working towards a goal for quite some time with little to no results? Is it a relationship that seems to be going nowhere? A job search that leads to dead ends or a familial relationship that remains toxic and strained?

Maybe the solution is to stop trying so hard and let go. Perhaps you need to step away from the situation and focus on other things. Up until this point, you have done everything you can to make it work.

Maybe it's time to let spirit take the reins while you observe what direction your life needs to go in. Relinquishing control, letting things settle, and being open to multiple outcomes can lead us where we need to be.

47

I AM RELEASING

Part of healing is moving on and learning to let go. Learn to release things that no longer work. Learn to say goodbye to what no longer supports you. By releasing the old, you embrace new opportunities. More is coming for you. It's a bright new beginning.

TIME FOR REFLECTION

Is there something you have been holding on to for far too long? Perhaps it is a relationship that is no longer working or closure you have been waiting for that never actually came. Maybe it's time to accept what is and understand that is your new reality. There is certainly a time for hoping and wishing. Positive thinking has a valid place in our lives, but when things are no longer moving, falling away, or stagnating, that is a signal from the universe to let it go.

Is there something that stopped moving in your life? Something you are still holding out hope for?

Make the decision to release it today and consider that better things are coming.

48

I AM POETRY

Spirit doesn't always speak in a direct way. Spirit speaks in dreams, riddles, and stories. Spirit speaks in music, sounds, and nature. At times it may be subtle, hidden beneath the bustle of life. We just have to attune our ears to hear the message. In order to hear spirit, we must slow down and look at the greater meaning behind ordinary things. There is a hidden message there if we take time to listen.

WRITE IT OUT

Spirit often speaks in dream language, which is poetry. They teach us through metaphors and parables, not always in a literal way. Take some time this week to record your dreams upon waking. You don't have to remember everything. It may come to you in bits and pieces. Write those bits and pieces down and reflect on the contents of the dream in your waking moments.

Do you dream of animals or long-lost family members?

Do you dream of past partners or friends?

All of these things are symbols that need to be interpreted.

Quietly ask yourself what each symbol means.

Wait for the answer and write it down.

This is how spirit speaks.

49

I AM SEEKING

Always be a student. Always be a seeker. Always be curious. When we admit that there is much we do not know, it opens us up to what could be. It opens us up to knowledge and new information. The more we are willing to seek, the more we are willing to learn. In turn, the more receptive we are to concepts and knowledge that enrich our lives. Everyone was a beginner once. A series of new beginnings ensures we keep growing. In growth and curiosity, there is great power.

TIME FOR REFLECTION

Think of a question you want to know the answer to. Make sure it is something that is important to you. Now, at the start of your day, ask spirit to reveal the answer to you as the day progresses. Be observant, and pay attention to signs and signals that cross your path.

Sometimes, conversations with strangers will reveal what you need to know. Other times it may come in the form of a song or be spelled out on a billboard. When we seek answers and desire the truth, spirit communicates with us. We just have to be open to the ways in which the messages come. There is always something new to learn and information waiting to be revealed.

50

I AM SOUL

You are eternal. The body may fade away, but the soul, the part of you that is immortal, will remain. You are pure energy. You can never be destroyed. You only change form. Embrace the goodness and resilience of your soul. The eternal part is what matters.

WRITE IT OUT

Take some time to embrace what you love about yourself. I don't mean your outer appearance. I mean your inner life. Your inner world.

Do you have a kindness about you or a resilience that is unmatched?

Does your creativity bring you joy?

Do you love others deeply?

All of these things are eternal qualities that reflect the beauty of the soul.

They can never be taken away or diminished.

What do you love about yourself that is eternal?

What do you love about yourself that is intangible?

Take a moment to write that out now.

51

I AM GRACE

Grace is not something you earn. It is something you are given. It is a sweet gift that you are born with. In grace lies protection and deep connection to the divine. In grace lies the ability to start over and the strength to forgive yourself and others. Grace can never be taken away. It affords us the ability to learn from our past mistakes and atone for the wrongs we have committed. It allows us patience and forgiveness for ourselves and others. We do not have to stay rooted in the past; we only have to see the message and shift the behavior. Grace allows us to do that.

TIME FOR REFLECTION

When you wake up today, take some time to be with the divine. Take some time to talk with God. Marvel at the miracle of life. You are alive and safe in this moment. The past is gone. The future has yet to be determined. In this time, in this quiet place, you are protected, loved, and whole.

Life is a miracle. You are a miracle, and by the grace of the Divine Creator, you have the ability to see this beautiful day and experience it once more. Grace moves through you. Grace surrounds you. Embrace the miracle of this moment. You are spirit in human form. You are supported and loved, no matter what.

Positive affirmation cards created by the author
that provided the inspiration for this book.

CONCLUSION

I hope you enjoyed this book, and that the positive affirmations have made a meaningful impact on your life. Always remember, this is a living work you can choose to revisit at any time. The purpose is to facilitate your healing and help you create the life you want. Continue to create new affirmations, exercises, and writing prompts of your own. Watch how beautifully things unfold. I am honored to be a part of your personal growth journey.

Keep going!

Transformation and change begin with one single step!

BIBLIOGRAPHY

67

Hay, Louise. *You Can Heal Your Life*. USA: Hay House Publishing, 1984.

ABOUT THE AUTHOR

Nicole Bowman is an award-winning psychic, medium, and intuitive artist. She is a graduate of New York University Tisch School of the Arts and a member of Shay Parker's Best American Psychics. Nicole is a recipient of the Social Activism Award from the Best American Psychics Organization. Her work has been featured in publications such as *Authority Magazine*, *Bustle*, *Cosmopolitan*, and *Refinery 29*. Nicole has also made appearances on programs including *Everyone Is Psychic*, *Nessa On Air*, and *Voxtur*. Always remember to live your light, live your bliss, and love yourself!